SAFARI

ROBERT BATEMAN

and Rick Archbold

A MADISON PRESS BOOK

produced for

LITTLE, BROWN AND COMPANY

First published in the United States by
Little, Brown and Company
Three Center Plaza
Boston, MA
02108-2084

First edition 1998

Library of Congress Cataloging-in-Publication Data

Bateman, Robert, 1930-
Safari / Robert Bateman. — 1st ed.
p.   cm.

Summary: Paintings and brief text present some of the animals found in Africa,
including elephants, giraffes, cheetahs, wildebeests, lions, and zebras.
ISBN 0-316-08265-1

1. Mammals—Africa—Juvenile literature. [1. Zoology—Africa.]
I. Archbold, Rick, 1950- . II. Title.
QL731.A1B38 1998
599'.096—dc21   98-6139

10 9 8 7 6 5 4 3 2 1

The works in this book, as well as other Robert Bateman paintings, have
been published as limited edition prints by Mill Pond Press. Please contact:
In the United States: Mill Pond Press Inc., 310 Center Court,
Venice, Florida 34292-3500   1-800-535-0331
In Canada: Nature's Scene, 976 Meyerside Drive, Unit 1, Mississauga,
Ontario L5T 1R9   1-800-387-6645

Design and Art Direction: Gordon Sibley Design Inc.
Editorial Director: Hugh M. Brewster
Project Editor: Mireille Majoor
Photography: Birgit Freybe Bateman
Consultant: Toby Styles, Toronto Zoo
Production Director: Susan Barrable
Production Co-ordinator: Sandra L. Hall
Color Separation: Colour Technologies
Printing and Binding: Artegrafica S.p.A.

SAFARI was produced by Madison Press Books,
which is under the direction of Albert E. Cummings

Produced by
Madison Press Books
40 Madison Avenue
Toronto, Ontario, Canada M5R 2S1

Printed and bound in Italy

For young people everywhere:
may you love nature — and protect it.

On Safari in Africa

In Africa there is a world that has hardly changed for hundreds of thousands of years. On a safari in an African game reserve you can see some of the largest animals left on earth. Groups of elephants and giraffes still roam across the plains. I have watched herds of antelope and zebra stretching as far as the eye could see.

Ever since I can remember, I have loved wild animals. I have traveled to almost every part of the globe to see them, to study them and to paint them. But I am always eager to return to Africa. Each time I visit, I discover something new — exactly how a giraffe runs, the way a lion stalks an antelope, where a gorilla makes its home.

A hundred years ago, the people who visited the African parks came to hunt big game. Hunters hoped to bring back lion skins or elephant tusks. Today, most people who come on safari bring cameras instead of guns and take home photographs instead of skins. I bring my sketchbook and fill it with drawings and ideas for new paintings.

On this safari, you will be a guest in an ancient world. Leave your modern life behind and listen to the rhythm of the land. If you are patient, and watch carefully, you will discover some of its secrets.

(Above) An orphan cheetah lets me sketch up close.

(Left) An impala portrait.

(Opposite top) Our Land Rover passes a herd of wildebeests.

(Opposite bottom) I draw a tame baby elephant.

Elephant

Elephants like to forage in forests where they can eat juicy young leaves and twigs from the treetops. You can hear them breaking off branches and munching. You can even hear the rumbling of their stomachs.

Because elephants are the largest land animals, they need to eat constantly. So an elephant herd is always on the move, looking for its next meal. A herd can travel as far as 40 miles (64 km) in one night.

No wonder elephants love to stop and cool down when they find water. In the heat of an African afternoon, one of the best places to look for elephants is at a watering hole or a river.

ELEPHANT

Habitat: Forests, grasslands, river valleys

Height: Up to 14 ft (4 m)

Weight: 7,000 – 13,500 lb (3,000 – 6,250 kg)

Food: Vegetation, including fruit, leaves, bark, grass

Range: Southern, central and eastern Africa

The leader of an elephant herd is always the oldest female, known as the matriarch. She remembers where the deepest water holes are and knows the best places to find food.

The face of one of these wise, old female elephants makes me think of a map. The creases and wrinkles are like the mountains and rivers. The flat places are the wide plains.

Young male elephants do not live with the females and calves. Instead, they roam together in small groups. Sometimes they test their strength by fighting with each other.

Leopard

O nce I saw a leopard that had been chased up a sausage tree by an angry lioness. The leopard had come too close to her cubs and then had to find the nearest place to escape. Luckily, the leopard is the best climber of all the big cats. This one looked relaxed as he lounged among the sausage-shaped fruit that gives this tree its name. Down below, the lioness snarled and thrashed her tail furiously. The leopard watched her for a few moments, then glided along the branch into another tree and disappeared.

Giraffe

The first time I saw a giraffe, I couldn't believe how tall it was. Even a six-month-old giraffe, like the one at right, is already over 10 feet (3 m) tall. What surprised me even more is how fast giraffes can run. With their slender legs and knobby knees, giraffes look as though they might trip over their own feet. Instead, they glide along as gracefully as ice skaters.

When I was painting the giraffes on the left, I tried to capture the elegant rocking motion they make as they run. First their front legs stretch forward. As their hooves touch the ground, their necks arch back. When their hind legs come forward, their necks go forward, too. It is almost like watching a herd of galloping rocking horses!

GIRAFFE

Habitat: Grassland

Height: Up to 18 ft (5.5 m)

Weight: Up to 3,000 lb (1,400 kg)

Food: Leaves and shoots

Range: Central, eastern and southern Africa

Wildebeest

Wildebeests travel across the African plains in huge herds of a thousand or more. I watched this group as they gathered together for the night. The setting sun cast a golden light over the long grass and the grazing animals. According to one African legend, God made the wildebeest out of the bits and pieces He had left over after He

finished creating all the other animals. He gave the wildebeest a mule's face, a cow's horns, a goat's beard, and a horse's body. Sometimes a wildebeest behaves as if all these bits and pieces want to go in different directions. It will start to gallop around, leap up and down, and kick its heels into the air for no reason we can see.

WILDEBEEST

Habitat: Grassy plains

Height: 4.5 ft (1.4 m)

Weight: Up to 600 lb (270 kg)

Food: Grass

Range: Central, eastern and southern Africa

Lion

The leader of a pride of lions is always a big male, like the one in the painting on the right. But it is usually the lionesses who do the hunting. The two lionesses in the painting above have caught sight of a small herd of wildebeests, one of their favorite foods. For the next few minutes, perhaps even for the next hour, they will move silently through long grasses almost the same color as their golden-brown coats. If the wildebeests don't see them, they may get close enough to attack.

LION

Habitat: Grassy plains, open woodlands

Height: 3 feet (90 cm)

Weight: 300 – 400 lb (135 – 180 kg)

Food: Antelope, zebra, wildebeest, ostrich

Range: South of the Sahara desert

A group of two or three lionesses will work together to stalk and kill a wildebeest. After the females finish hunting, the male lion will appear. A lioness may snarl at him to keep him away, as shown below, but in the end she usually lets him take his share. I watched the three females in the bottom painting at sunset as they began to eat a wildebeest they had killed. The next morning they came back to finish the leftovers.

Cape Buffalo

A male Cape buffalo is the most dangerous of all African animals, especially if you find one by himself. Bulls sometimes charge at humans for no apparent reason. The Cape buffalo is such a powerful fighter that the only other African animal that will ever dare to challenge one is the lion.

But the Cape buffalo will not usually attack people and it is possible to get close to a grazing herd. A herd of Cape buffalo acts very much like a herd of cattle. They are curious about humans but don't see them as threats. The buffalo just munch their food while white cattle egrets hunt for insects stirred up by buffalo hooves.

CAPE BUFFALO

Habitat: Savannas and forests

Height: Up to 5.5 ft (1.7 m)

Weight: Up to 1,500 lb (680 kg)

Food: Grass, leaves, herbs

Range: South of the Sahara desert

Zebra and Lesser Kudu

It seems amazing that an animal covered with black and white stripes would be hard to see against the golden grasses of the African plains. But from a distance it is very difficult to spot a zebra. Its pattern of dark and light stripes tricks you into thinking you're seeing light and shadows in the grass instead of an animal.

Other animals have more obvious camouflage. When the lesser kudu is standing still, its stripes look like the branches of trees. In fact most animals, whether they are the hunters or the hunted, can blend into the landscape when they want to stay hidden.

Habitat: ZEBRA: Grassy plains; KUDU: Dry thornbush areas, open forest

Height: ZEBRA: Up to 4.5 ft (1.35 m); KUDU: Up to 3.7 ft (1.1 m)

Weight: ZEBRA: Up to 660 lb (300 kg); KUDU: Up to 230 lb (105 kg)

Food: ZEBRA: Grasses; KUDU: Leaves, herbs, grasses, fruit

Range: ZEBRA: Eastern and southern Africa; KUDU: Eastern Africa

Cheetah

The cheetah is the fastest animal on land and can run up to 60 miles per hour (96 kilometers per hour). But it can only run that quickly over a short distance, so a cheetah has to get very close to an antelope before it can attack. An antelope can't run quite as fast as a cheetah, but it can keep running for much longer. If an antelope gets a head start, it can usually escape.

A cheetah's teeth are not as sharp as a lion's or a leopard's, and its jaws are not as strong. If a lion or a leopard comes along when a cheetah is eating, the cheetah won't put up a fight. It will just move away and let one of the bigger cats finish its meal.

CHEETAH

Habitat: Open country

Height: Up to 3 feet (1 m)

Length: 6 feet (2 m) including tail

Weight: Up to 100 lb (45 kg)

Food: Small animals, including antelope, hares, birds, young ostriches

Range: South of the Sahara desert

Dik-Dik and Impala

A full-grown dik-dik is barely taller than the pile of elephant dung in this painting. It is one of the smallest members of the antelope family, only growing about one foot (30 cm) high. A dik-dik can spend its whole life in an area the size of a city block. Like a rabbit, it moves quickly and freezes the moment it senses danger. Then all that stand out are the dik-dik's big, dark eyes.

DIK·DIK

Habitat: Bush country with thick undergrowth, scattered trees

Height: Up to 12 inches (30 cm)

Weight: Up to 14 lb (6.5 kg)

Food: Leaves, shoots, fruit

Range: Eastern and southwestern Africa

Because its eyes are on either side of its long head, the dik-dik can see behind itself without turning.

Beside a huge, old baobab tree, the two impala bucks in this painting look tiny. But even though they are close relatives, an

IMPALA	
Habitat:	Dry forests, mountains, plains
Height:	Up to 3.1 ft (95 cm)
Weight:	Up to 175 lb (80 kg)
Food:	Grass, leaves, fruit
Range:	Eastern and southern Africa

impala is several times the size of a dik-dik.

If you look closely at the baobab tree, you will see that much of the bark is missing. Elephants use their tusks to tear off long strips. Baobab bark is one of the elephant's favorite foods.

Robert Bateman

Rhinoceros

With its thick armor plates and dangerous-looking horn, the rhinoceros seems like a creature from a science-fiction movie. But its hide is made of tightly woven hair and its horn is formed from the same material as human fingernails.

This horn is the reason the rhinoceros may soon disappear. There are people who believe the rhino's horn can make men more powerful and cure sickness. Some hunters kill rhinos for their valuable horns alone.

Unfortunately, it's easy for hunters to get close to rhinos because these animals have such bad eyesight. On safari this can also cause some exciting moments. If a rhino starts moving in your direction, it may run right over you before it even sees you.

RHINOCEROS	
Habitat:	Grassy plains
Height:	Up to 6 feet (1.8 m)
Weight:	Up to 3,000 lb (1,360 kg)
Food:	Leaves of shrubs and bushes
Range:	South of the Sahara desert

Gorilla

To visit the gorillas, I left the open plains and traveled to the dense jungle. On one trip with my whole family, we hiked through the hot, damp rain forest, climbing over slippery roots, through mud and stinging nettles. Suddenly we saw them — a family of gorillas resting at the edge of a clearing. We quickly lay down like the gorillas and pretended to sleep in the warm sun.

After a while the young gorillas became curious about us. First one, then another rolled and somersaulted in our direction. But when one of them came too close, the big male gorilla, who was the head of the family, grunted a warning. The youngster instantly somersaulted away. After half an hour or so, naptime was over. The gorilla family stretched and yawned. Soon they vanished back into the jungle and we quietly crept away.

GORILLA

Habitat: Mountain rain forest

Height: 5 – 6 ft (1.5 – 1.8 m)

Weight: 200 – 400 lb (90 – 180 kg)

Food: Fruit, roots, leaves, bark

Range: Central and western Africa

Photo by Gary Fiegehen

Saving Wild Places

In every country there are fewer and fewer truly wild places where plants and animals can live as they always have. No wonder the game reserves of Africa seem so special.

But, unless we work together to protect the wilderness that is left, many of the animals in this book may soon disappear. Rhinos are hunted for their horns. Elephants are killed for their valuable ivory tusks. Every year there are fewer of these and other African animals roaming the game reserves.

We can only stop the uncontrolled killing if we learn to live in harmony with nature, like the native Africans, who have lived with the lions, the rhinos, and the vast herds of antelope for hundreds of thousands of years.